ALL ABOUT ME
Reflections of Life Experiences

A COLLECTION OF POEMS, SHORT STORIES, SONG LYRICS, AND QUOTES

WRITTEN By,

Ms. Lashawn Chevalier

Copy @ Date_____

Contents

About the Author

Lashawn Theresa Chevalier was born in New Orleans, Louisiana. She came to Los Angeles, California, when she was 19 years of age, where she still resides today. She attended Los Angeles Southwest College, where she took a class in creative writing, wrote for the school newspaper, and received an AA Degree in the study of Sociology. From there, she went on to continue her education at California State University, Dominigue Hills. She received the degree of Bachelor of Arts in Human Services. She attended an additional two years at CSUDH in a master's degree program, studying for a dual master's degree in clinical psychology and Marriage and Family Counseling.

Miss Chevalier worked in health care for several years, including owner and operator of Orchid Medical Supplies & Equipment, located in Inglewood California.

Dedication

First and utmost I thank God for blessing me with the ability to

Write this book. And I thank everyone who purchases a copy.

With my deepest gratitude, I thank my 2 sons, George and Clayton

For their encouragement to complete this book.

I also thank my niece and coach, Robin, who was one of my biggest supporters

(www.COACHINGBYROBIN>COM).

And a special thanks goes to my niece Stacie and my friend Jack, who supported me by keeping my Tech working. I thank my prayer partners, Hybebah (sister) and Lisa Bordere (niece).

And finally, my two new friends and mentors, Jurline Redeaux, Author

Of Conversations With Mom, and Gloria Ewing Lockhart, Author of

Unmasking, A Women's Journey.

Preface

I first started writing poetry when I was in the fourth grade. On my first day of school, our class assignment was to go to the library and find a poem to recite the following day. Of course, I decided to write my own poem, and when I presented it to the class, the whole class laughed. The embarrassment was almost overwhelming.

However, the teacher scolded the class for laughing and praised me for using my creativity to write my own poem. At that time, I felt a sense of shy-confidence. Of course, I continued to write my poems, only not so willing to share.

I wrote my first short story when I was in the fifth grade. It was about aliens from out of space, but I got so scared after reading it that I tore it up. Ha, Ha.

Introduction

In writing this book of poems, short stories, song lyrics, and quotes. My goal is to capture the many feelings, moments, and thoughts that makeup life. I hope you, the readers, will enjoy reading this book. And that you will find humor, be inspired, and know that as part of humanity, we all share some of the same emotions.

Although the world consists of trillions of people. Sometimes, we feel we are the only ones in the world experiencing our own experiences. May it be Joy, Sadness, grief, disappointment, solitude, or unnatural experiences.

SECTION I
Poems

CONTENTS: SECTION I

Contents: Section I Cont.

ADMIRATION

Admiration at its highest,

You do deserve.

You are a survivor of the fittest,

I have watched you survive,

Through storms of:

Illness,

Displacement,

And disappointment,

Each time coming out on Top of the hill.

Lead by your spiritual self.

You had God by your side all the way,

I do believe.

So, I say to you, my special sister,

Only look back at your accomplishments,

Which are many.

And don't look back at stormy times,

For they no longer matter.

I love you, Hybebah.

AWAITING

Today,

An extension of yesterday,

And a part of tomorrow,

Awaiting to fall into place.

Like a rose petal in the spring,

A multicolored leaf in the fall,

Winter's cold breath,

And Summer's sunshine,

Awaiting to fall into place,

Just awaiting.

Be Grateful for The Now

In the midst of the night,

Swallowed up by solitude,

Tranquility is the ultimate resolution.

Forget about yesterday,

And remember not too long tomorrow.

Just be grateful for the now.

For yesterday has drifted away,

Beyond reach.

And tomorrow is yet too far to be a promise.

California Scammers

Scammers just waiting at the bus stops.

With smiling faces,

Welcoming,

Newcomers,

All day long.

Selling dream tickets,

Buy 3, get 1 free,

What Ch Wanna Be?

Leaving your own hometown,

Where opportunities failed to exist.

So, you ran as fast as you could to a new world.

While you were still too young to make a comparison,

To what really counts.

You seek excitement, riches, and fame.

But you don't really know their names.

Your admiration for opportunities began to fade,

It's just too many games being played,

And the few trinkets you pocketed in the past,

All turned to sand compared to what you had.

In that small town called home that you once had.

Exceeded

Self-motivated,

I exceeded my own exportations,

In spite of the non-inspirations,

I had people say

I was reaching too high

While I only wanted to reach for the sky

Some said I didn't have what it takes,

So, I lead my own path,

And I went on my way,

And then one day,

Maybe even today,

I can look back and say

I have touched the sky,

And I am still on my way.

Expensive

The most expensive things of all.'

In the universe,

Are free,

Sometimes you have

More than what you need,

And sometimes not enough.

So, when you spend it,

Spend it wisely,

Only give it to those who,

You love and trust,

Or those you think need it the most.

You can share it with your family and friends,

But always keep some,

On hand for yourself.

Try not to use it,

On things that shouldn't matter,

And only use it when you must.

Because your,

"TIME"

Is too expensive to waste.

Happy Birthday

Happy Birthday,

I am sorry,

I am late.

Next year we will celebrate.

We will have a great time,

It will be a great day,

All this will be behind you,

Great days await.

You will have a great life,

And a beautiful daughter that waits,

So, remember to always,

Keep up the faith.

I love you,

Happy Birthday,

I am sorry,

I am late.

HAPPY TO BE BACK

So happy to be back on track again.

Life was a struggle,

With so much pain.

Feeling left behind, and

Humiliated at times.

With nothing to do,

And nowhere to go,

Just watching the world,

Passing by so slow.

Always looking for a higher high,

And adapting to so many self-lies.

There was always a reason to want to get high.

With no one to help,

You silently cried,

Desperately wanting not to get high.

But that revolving door,

Continued to turn you around.

Wanting to get off,

But not knowing how.

Until the day came that you knew

You would die,

If you didn't get off that roller coaster ride.

It wasn't easy,

It was damn hard at times,

But with self-determination,

You made it back just in time.

Now you can look in the mirror,

And know your own name.

Giving God the credit,

You are sober and sane.

And knowing you will never go back there again,

So happy to be a part of life again.

He Was a Nephew of Mine

As a brilliant young man barely of age.'

He left his boy-size boots at home.'

To serve his country as a man.

Although he didn't go to war,

He returned home completely.

Traumatized and depleted,

Of whom he once was,

When he left his hometown.

He had a brilliant mind,

Which should have never been left behind.

When he first returned home,

He was still marching in a straight line.

As though it had been imprinted in his mind.

I think of him often,

He was a nephew of mine.

And I wonder what could have happened,

To such a brilliant mind.

I wonder what could have happened.

To a man that didn't go to war,

Yet still came back,

So confused and so lost.

He came home with so many meds,

In and out of the hospital,

So many times,

He was a vet,

And everyone knew his name.

He was a nephew of mine,

With a brilliant mind.

Oh, How Vivid are the Days of Yesteryears

Oh, how vivid are the days of yesteryears,

Of not so long ago,

When flying kites,

And school days were all we knew.

When hiding the teacher's hall passes,

Running through the school halls,

And being mischievous,

Was so much fun.

When parties and talking on the telephone,

Was primary of them all.

Oh, how vivid are the days of yesteryears,

Of not so long ago.

I can almost still smell,

Mama's fried chicken,

On Sunday mornings.

And getting up late for church,

Knowing I would still have to go.

Oh, how vivid are the days of yesteryears,

Of not so long ago.

When New Orleans was a place I called home,

And Mardi Gras was the day,

You got to be,

Who even you wanted to be,

All year long.

Oh, how vivid are the days of yesteryears,

Of not so long ago.

Mama moved to heaven,

Just a few years ago.

Now, New Orleans is just a place,

I used to call home.

Oh, how vivid are the days of yesteryears,

Of not so long ago.

I ALMOST FORGOT

Oh, I almost forgot about yesterday,

The days I never wanted to forget,

The days when dreams developed,

And love existed,

A place where time stood still,

And stability was the norm.

Oh, I almost forgot to remember,

A time when I thought the people closest to me,

Would always be there.

A time before death became a reality,

And time moved on.

Oh, I almost forgot to remember,

What I never wanted to forget.

2/22/2012

I AM PROUD

My blackness lies Beneath my skin,

But it is still there,

Never denied,

I am like an Oreo cookie,

Inside out.

I have been mistaken for,

Spanish,

Asian,

And mixed Caucasian.

But I know who I am.

I am a proud black woman.

With values that lie beneath my skin,

Which tells me every day,

I am black,

I am beautiful.

I am proud.

I am me.

I have witnessed prejudice,

From every side,

Including family and friends,

And I didn't know why,

I was too black,

Or too much from the other side.

Sometimes it even made me cry.

But I know who I am,

I am a black woman with pride.

I Have Everything I Need

I don't have everything I want,

But I have everything I need.

I have food in the fridge.

The lights are on.

A roof over my head,

And a place called home.

Clothes to wear,

Not so new,

They will keep me warm,

so I guess they will do.

I have shoes to wear,

That will take me a mile,

And a beautiful sunshine to make me smile.

I don't have everything I want.

But I have everything I need.

I want a million dollars,

Or a trillion,

The latter will do.

But I only need a hundred or two.

Some mornings, I wake up with arthritis pain,

Some mornings, I wake up feeling like 16 again.

My car broke down 16 times last year,

I don't know how far it will go this year.

The air conditioning went out,

Two years ago,

The heater a month,

Or two, or more.

But it still gets me everywhere I want to go.

And I still have a car to get to the store.

So, I'll say once more,

I don't have everything I want,

But I have everything I need.

INVENT YOUR OWN VAMPIRE

Go ahead and invent your own vampire,

And be indebted until death do you part.

I often wonder what could have persuaded you to sign,

Your own imaginary dream certificate,

Your own pain certificate,

Your own death certificate.

Didn't you know you could have gotten the same effects,

From wine and sex.

Did you ever wonder what your children would do?

Will they become survivors of your past,

Or will they, too,

Follow your tracks,

And invent their own vampires.

IT's TIME TO BE ME

Insecure and frail,

In a vulnerable state of mind.

I just wanted to run away,

So, I did,

within my own mind.

Now I must go back,

And reclaim me,

Still not wanting to be,

I have already lost my identity.

Time has sent me through a windpool,

Across the galaxy,

So far out, so fast, so free.

But now it's time to come back.

It's time to be me.

Joy To My World

My biggest Joy in life,

Watching my two boys grow up.

And although they were years apart,

I loved them each just as much.

I often look back at the day they were born,

And all the joy they brought into my life,

When I brought them into my world.

And now that they are grown,

I am so proud to say,

I love the men that they have become:

Kind and Courageous,

Brilliant and Strong.

And I love them every day.

JUDGED

Judged for who you were,

And who you weren't,

By Family, Friends, and sometimes strangers,

With small points of view.

With secrets in their own closets, I wonder who you are.

Yet, refuse to judge, the judges, for what good would
that do.

Better to move on without them,

And just be a better you.

Life is a Cycle

Life is a cycle that must go on,

I am on my way out,

I just can't stay,

Life just wasn't made that way.

I have experienced a full cycle of life,

I've had my turn,

And life was like a beautiful song,

Most of my family is now gone,

All waiting for me,

With a beautiful song.

I tell them not to sweat,

It won't be long,

I've had my turn.

Now, the next generation,

Must have their turn.

For life is a cycle that must go on.

LIFE ITSELF

I am about 2/3 from my destine,

I hope I'll make it all the way.

Only heaven knows the distance,

I just know I am on my way.

The journey I'll be leaving behind,

Was great,

I have encountered many blessings,

A few mishaps,

That I never understood,

However, life has its ups and downs,

And most of it was good.

I apologize to no one,

I am leaving behind,

But if someone thinks I owe them one,

I might understand,

If I knew why.

A MOTHER'S PAIN

He walked the streets of L.A.,

No one knowing where,

And in the many days of not knowing why,

His mother cried,

As she prayed to God,

To find her sweet child.

Then, one day,

Out of the blue,

She got a call,

And it was from her sweet child.

They reunited,

For three years long,

And every day was like a sweet song.

She thanked Jesus for sending her sweet child home.

But as the years began to unfold.

The time came when Jesus called her sweet child home.

And although her heart was broken that day.

She knows he now walks the streets of sweet heaven,

And with loved ones on the other side,

Is where he is today.

Now, looking back at yesteryear,

She'll never forget the precious gift of three years' time,

She was given the day her sweet child was found.

And the sweet memories they shared will always be there.

Although she will miss him every day.

The love between them will always stay.

LONG LIFE

I have a little story.

That should have long been told,

We all know this story well,

But no one wants it to be told.

Everyone wants a long life,

But no one wants to get old,

But how can you have a long life,

Without getting old.

If your journey takes you there

Celebrate every birthday,

And be grateful to get old.

You will have wisdom to spare.

And stories to share.

And memories of all the good times you had.

SAD GIRLS

Girls on the streets from broken homes or no homes at
all.

Confidence and self-esteem, torn and ripped apart.

Which should have been theirs to keep.

Just waiting to be found,

One day

Someday,

Somehow.

For now, just another day trying to survive.

I tell you, never give up your hope and drive to strive,

Look into the mirrors of your mind and see beyond your
sad eyes.

Look for your beauty, from inside out and outside in,

Reclaim your confidence and self-esteem.

It's always been there,

Yours to keep.

Sad girls, you don't belong on the streets.

She's My Sister

She's her own person,

Strange at times,

Who cares? She's my sister.

She loves to tell you what to do,

Are what not to do.

Her motto might be,

A penny saved is a penny well spent.

And if she hears about a food,

Without calories or taste,

She will recommend it to her sisters,

Who doesn't worry about their waist,

But she's my sister.

She's beautiful, smart and witty.

And she tries to be a part,

Of everyone's business,

No matter the cost.

But she's my sister,

And I love her very much.

I love you, Anna (8/30/13)

SIDEWALK NEIGHBORHOODS

Sidewalks becoming neighbors.

With no addresses,

People pushed from street to street,

With no place to go.

So, they return later,

Just to start over,

Bringing with them their worn-out belongs,

All are collected on trash day.

They rebuild their sidewalk homes.

With cardboard boxes and broken pieces of wood, with

broken hearts and being misunderstood.

They are individuals like me and you,

Taxpayers from years ago,

Now left without jobs,

And nowhere to go.

The availability of humanitarian effects

Came all too late.,

So now the sidewalks are where they stay.

TIME AND SPACE

Somewhere between time and space.'

Is all I need to be found.

I keep looking,

But it's too hard to find time.

There is just too much space.

Welcomed by the State

People entering from other countries,

Bring their own survival skills,

Displaced, misplaced,

Just another new face,

Trying to adapt to a new place.

Being cared for by the state,

Humanitarian services await,

At the entry gate.

People in our own country,

Are also displaced,

And wait,

And wait,

At the back of the line,

And for humanitarian services,

They, too, are still waiting.

Yes, take care of as many people,

That are displaced, if we can,

But don't forget the faces,

In your own land.

.

WHO MIGHT SHE BE

Looking at a photo of a little girl

6 or 7, she might be.

All dressed up on communion day,

Her face has no expression

sadly to say.

It really should be a happy day,

I wonder what she might say,

I wonder why so sad on such a happy day,

I can see a little fear of what the day might be,

She quietly copes with denial,

And sometimes unbelief,

which she'll carry throughout her life,

That's just the way it had to be

She selectively forgets the harsh times,

whenever needed to be.

Her defenses are magnificent,

It's how she learned to be,

and though I wonder who she was,

I think she might be me.

WILLOW TREE

Shattered memories lie,

Beneath the willow tree.

I am just a child,

This shouldn't be.

My father lies just beneath,

The willow tree.

I am told he is resting,

But how can this be?

Moving on beyond my years,

Almost forgotten, yet always near.

How do you forget the willow tree,

When you know, your father lies just beneath.

I remember the day he left,

Without saying goodbye

I was so in shock,

I couldn't cry.

Everyone was so apart,

There was no one to comfort my bleeding heart.

A Letter to My Sister

Missing you, missing you, Missing you

Where did all the time go?

You always had so much to do,

You were busier than anyone I knew.

I never thought you would have to go,

You helped more people than you'll ever know,

your rosier became like a daily song,

Even when times were low, your faith was strong,

God gave you the strength to live and die,

Now, every day,

You're gone, I cry.

You were the strength of our family,

Although I am strong enough to abide,

I'd rather sit here and cry.

TO MY SISTER JEANNETTE

I knew her story.

I knew her life, she was my sister,

So beautiful and bright.

She had a smile that would light up the night.

As your light started to dim,

From pain and despair,

God took your hand with love and care.

I know you must have celebrated the night,

With so many awaiting to greet you that night.

Your mom and dad, so happy and glad,

To see you that night.

And Rickie and Michael with so much delight.

Your brothers Walter and Raymond,

With a smile so bright.

And don't forget your sisters, Voilet and Deanna,

Who probably gave you a hug that night.

Although I will miss you,

From this side of the light,

I love you, dear sister,

I love you,

Good Night

To My Sister Kim

I want to write about you,

But I don't know what to say.

You left so unexpectedly,

The doors didn't close all the way.

You left a void in my heart,

And I miss you every day.

You were always a good listener.

And you prayed every day,

You were always my big sister,

And sometimes my mother too.

I can't think of any days,

You were not there when I needed you.

Except for now,

When I am so much missing you.

ROBOTIC SELF

You engineered your own,

Robotic self.

Designed to forget,

How you obtained your pain.

So, you shout out in anger,

Hoping to be heard,

Without being noticed.

Hoping to be looked at,

But not seen.

You wanted to find a way,

To redesign your make-up,

Because your biological heart,

Just couldn't take the pain.

So, you continue to function,

Best you can,

Noticed for your anger,

But not your pain.

SECTION II
SHORT
STORIES

CONTENTS: SECTION II

SHORT STORIES:

LIFE AFTER LIFE

Throughout the ages, there have been believers and non- believers of life after life.

As I write my own story, I know there will be some who will believe and some that will not. I chose not to judge either side. I only ask that you keep an open mind.

I chose not to identify with death, after life, because I believe only the body dies in death, not the mind. In my own mind I feel certain there is another side to life after death. I am basing my theory on the unnatural experiences I had in my own life through my childhood dreams.

The first dream that I can remember is of an elderly lady with a large black hat. In the dream, the lady asked me to tell my mom something. I don't remember the message at this time; however, when I described the lady to my mom and gave her the message, she knew who I was talking about. It was a relative who had passed years before my time. Another time, when I was a child, I dreamed of a little girl with a long black ponytail around my age. In the dream, we played all day and were having a lot of fun. And then she became ill and died. I remember waking up very sad as if it had really happened. When I told my mom about the dream I had and described the little girl, she said I described her little sister who had played all day and became ill that evening and passed away at 9 years old.

When I was about 7 years old, a lady named Sally lived a couple of houses down from my house. We became friends, and I visited her whenever I saw her sitting on her porch. One Saturday, while spending the night at a friend's house. I had a dream that my friend Sally had passed away. Strangely, when I got home the next day, my mother informed me of Sally's death. When we went to her house for her viewing, her casket was on the right side of the room, and everything was exactly as it was in my dream.

Just a few years ago, a friend of mines informed me of her brother's passing and how she wished she had talked to him before he had passed. At that point, I told her about my past dream experiences. And I asked her if she would like me to try to contact him through a dream. She showed me a picture of him, which I used to focus on before I went to bed. As a result, when I went to sleep, I dreamed I was in a very cold place, in an alley where a group of ladies was standing around a tall tin can on fire, trying to keep warm. Across from the alley I could hear extremely loud music playing, then I saw her brother walking up a green stairway towards an apartment. I asked him if he could give me a message to give to his sister. He said to tell her I was okay. The next day when I talked to my friend. She informed me that her brother had lived in Chicago, where he played in a band inside a bar, and the music was always extremely loud.

I also remember when waking up from this dream I was so cold I was shivering. The dream was so real I decided to never try this again, and I have never sensed it.

I did not always believe in the life after life. It all started when I lost a close relative. Who died in a car accident. A week after his service, I had a dream of him riding on a large white unicorn. In the dream, he said he had been to everyone in the family, looking for someone to give his mother a message for him. Then, he spoke in a language that I didn't understand. And because I didn't understand the message. I didn't relate the dream I had to his mother until a month later. Surprisingly, she fully understood the message. She said before his fatal accident, they had discussed in length that he believed in tongues.

A couple of years after that experience, I had a dream of my niece, who had recently passed. In this dream, my niece looked so beautiful. She said do not be afraid when it's your time to go, because it is very beautiful here. Then she asked if I would ask her brother to forgive her for something she had done to him years ago and to tell him she was very sick at that time. When I spoke to her brother regarding the dream, He did not go into detail about the message. However, he said he knew exactly what she was talking about.

There are many other unnatural experiences I have had through dreams which occurred throughout the years. However, just too many to share at this time.

I believe there are many other individuals just like myself, who encounter. Unnatural experiences. However, because they are unaware. Or non-believers, they look for explanations for their unnatural experiences. And when they are not logical, they assume that they are just coincidences. Although they may or may not be.

A Birthday Letter to My Brother

Dear Billy,

Just wanted you to know although I don't call as much as I should, I think of you often. I have such good memories of you when I was a child. The best is when I hated when you teased me by calling me by that nickname I hated (you know, the one). I would be walking from school with friends, and when I saw that red truck you drove, I would cover my face with my books, hoping you didn't see me, not realizing that hiding my face is what made me stand out. There came that nickname again with a loud laugh. I could still hear the laughter; I would get so upset. Who would have thought those memories would now be cherished and loved as good memories of my childhood.

Oh, I also remember how I was envious of your blue eyes, I just couldn't understand why God gave you the blue eyes instead of me. I remember telling you one day, I wish I had your blue eyes; and you said, no, you don't. I can't see a thing out of them. However, I didn't care; I still wanted them.

Now, not so sure; I went to Costco's and bought myself a pair of the same color, blue. So, dear brother, thank you for all the good memories you gave me while growing up. There were many others, but these were my favorite. Love You, Happy Birthday, from your sister Lashawn.

1/15/2019.

CRAZE/HAPPY/SAD

Craze, happy, sad, is how I think of you. So happy to be in charge of your own life. Knowing that growing up was not easy. I feel sad when looking back at your childhood, Knowing your closest family and friends were your cats. In which they often sleep beneath the staircase outside your home. I often wonder how you even survived through All the humiliation, abuse, and no one to celebrate your birthdays because they were all cancelled.

I admire you because you made it through. Although crazy, happy, sad, is how I think of you. It is amazing how you integrated your daymares into crazy, funny jokes. Which we laughed at for hours on. You are so fun to be around. You could teach classes on how to survive, abandoned as a child.

My Best friend when I was 6.

At age 6, a time when children had lots of friends their own age.

My best friend was an old lady who lived around the corner from my house.

Her name was Mary; of course, she was Miss Mary to me.

Mary had a large pecan tree in her backyard. One day, I knocked on her door and asked if I could pick some pecans, and we became friends at this time. Out of all the kids in the neighborhood, I was the only kid she would let come into her yard and pick pecans. I think it was because I was the only kid who would ask her if I could pick pecans. I would pick pecans for her, too, and we would always talk for a while. I remember asking her how she got so old and if I was going to get old, too.

She always laughed at my questions. What I loved most about her is that she was the only one I could ask questions, she would listen and answer them. I think she looked forward to my visits, with my silly questions, and I listened to her stories, too. Mary was a very kind, caring, compassionate person.

One year, when Thanksgiving was approaching. I went to Mary's house, and she had a large duck roaming around her yard. I loved that duck so much that I gave it a name. Every day after school, I would go to Mary's house to play with the duck. I had so much fun chasing the duck around the yard.

Just a day or two before Thanksgiving, I went to Mary's house; Mary was in her yard, sitting in front of a pail of white feathers. I had no idea where the feathers had come from. However, I looked all over the yard for the duck but could not find him. When I told Mary, I couldn't find the duck. She said the duck had run away.

After a few days had passed and I still couldn't find the duck, I thought the Duck had just found another home. I gave up looking for the duck. I decided to go back to picking pecans. When I went behind the shade to pick up pecans. I found a pile of white feathers. I assumed the cat had eaten the duck. I was very disappointed.

I didn't tell Mary because I didn't want her to know the cat had eaten the duck.

In Essence, Mary told me the duck ran away to spare my feelings and

I didn't tell her the cat had eaten the duck to spare her feelings. I didn't realize.

Until years later, the white feathers in the pail were the duck. And the Duck became. Mary's enjoyable holiday dinner.

By Lashawn Chevalier

8/25/2023

SECTION III
SONG LYRICS

CONTENTS:
SECTION III

SONG LYRICS:

I had a dream last night

I had a dream

last night

that I got married

But it wasn't to

You, You, You

it was to someone else

I had a dream

last night

that I got married

But it wasn't to

You, You, You

It was to someone else

We had the largest Party,

And I was dressed so nice,

But   I was sorry, I had gotten married,

To someone else.

So I searched throughout the party

to find you.

I wanted to see your face for the last time,

I had something to tell you,

but I couldn't find you through the crowd,

I had a dream

last night,

that I got married,

But it wasn't to

You, You, You

It was to someone else,

In the end, I couldn't find you,

so I cried,

because I wanted to tell you,

that I still loved you

And I was sorry I married someone else,

There is only One Me

I heard your girlfriend,

Looks a lot like me.

She colored her hair,

And had surgery.

But with all the changes to impersonate me,

She just doesn't have the personality.

Although she walks behind me,

In all the world,

There is only one me,

There is only one me.

I heard your girlfriend,

Looks a lot like me,

I wonder if she wants to be me.

She doesn't know the story behind me.

And if she did,

She wouldn't want to be me.

I've had trials and tribulations.

Up to my knees,

There were times I thought I would never make it,

But in the end, I was,

Still me.

And yes, there were great times too,

And that is the reason she can't be me.

In essence, there is only one me.

We The People"

The world is a beautiful place

But not for everyone in it

We have a president who doesn't love

We, the people,

He'd rather make power,

for himself,

than abide by the pledge of allegiance

People dying from drugs, instead of helping,

people rather judge.

The world is beautiful,

but not for everyone in it

Families going against each other,

Where is the peace and love,

they once had for one another

The world is a beautiful place,

But not for everyone in it.

Politicians selling promises during elections,

Only to forget them,

if they are elected.

The world is beautiful,

but not for everyone in it,

Little children being abused by their parents,

The monsters that are supposed to be outside,

are really in.

The world is beautiful,

But not for everyone in it,

The power stricken,

The abusers,

and the unequalized,

voices should be deleted,

We, the people, should find ways,

to make the world beautiful,

for everyone in it.

END OF THE LINE

You were a player, in fact,

But now you met your match,

As a matter of fact,

You are at the end of the line.

You are still looking around,

To see who you can con,

But if you look into the mirror,

You'll see,

You are at the end of the line.

You were a player, in fact,

But now you met your match.

A little young thing,

Pretty and fine,

Now all she wants is your money,

Cause she can tell,

You are at the end of the line.

Your third stick used to be sharp and stiff.

Now, your stick is made of wood or pine,

You not only need it to walk,

But you are almost blind.

Yes, you used to be a player in fact,

Years ago, when your hair was still black.

Now that you have met your match,

Your hair looks like Silva Dollars,

To younger eyes,

Cause it's no longer black,

And you are at the end of the line.

For all the degrading you did,

While popping your whip,

Now you are feeling like,

You are getting whipped.

Because now you are at the end of the line.

End of the line,

End of the line,

End of the line.

The World Is Too Technical, Where did all the love go?

Right now, want to move on,

Got to move on,

Don't know which way to go.

Just can't keep up with technology anymore.

My brains are saturated with bull shit,

Fascinated with the new toys,

I Phones do everything,

But love you back.

The high cost of living keeps going up,

Yet we still struggle,

To buy the technical.

Right now, want to move on,

Got to move on,

Don't know which way to go.

The world is too technical,

Where did all the love go?

What happened to all the love songs?

From way back,

Now, all you here are,

F this,

And F that.

What happened to all the love in the world?

It's become too technical for emotions to play a part.

Text or Email,

Instead of talking.

There is no time,

To hear your voice,

Or feel the emotions of your heart,

That's why lovers keep falling apart,

Marriages don't last,

Engagements are a thing of the past.

Want to move on,

Got to move on,

Don't know which way to go.

Just can't keep up with technology anymore.

03/06/201

SECTION IV
QUOTES

CONTENTS: SECTION IV

A Little Versus A Lot

It is better to have a little bit of everything,

than a lot of nothing.

HATE DRUGS

Don't hate people who use drugs,

Hate drugs that use people.

LOVE ALWAYS

Love is like a scientific method,

It has no absolute truth.

And always cannot be measured,

Or taken for granted.

POSITIVITY

There is a positive outcome,

For every negative thought,

If you don't give in,

Or give up.

SOLITUDE VERSUS ATTITUDE

Solitude is always better than,

Attitude.

DON'T COMPROMISE

Don't compromise your pride,

For dollar signs.

Money can never withstand the signs of time.

Made in the USA
Las Vegas, NV
25 May 2024

90355225R00052